The Truth About the
New Covenant

10 Myths
of Modern Christianity

By Karajah Yashar

BLACKSTONE PUBLISHING

Batan Rouge, LA

The Truth About the New Covenant
10 Myths of Modern Christianity

www.bspbooks.com

ISBN: 978-1-962691-31-4

First Edition: June 2024

Table of Contents

Introduction: Rediscovering the Essence of the New Covenant

For centuries, believers have sought to understand and live out the teachings of Jesus Christ, often relying on traditions handed down through generations. These traditions, while deeply rooted in faith and community, have sometimes obscured the true essence of the New Covenant. This book aims to peel back the layers of historical and doctrinal developments to uncover the original intent and practice of the early church.

Tradition and Transformation

Traditions play a crucial role in shaping our understanding of faith. They provide continuity, a sense of belonging, and a framework within which believers can practice their faith. However, traditions can also become rigid, perpetuating practices and beliefs that may not align with the original teachings of Jesus or the experiences of the early church. Over time, these traditions can obscure the transformative message of the New Covenant, which is centered on a dynamic and personal relationship with God through Jesus Christ.

The Early Church: A Model for Modern Faith

The early church represents a period of profound spiritual awakening and growth. It was a time when the followers of Jesus, guided by the apostles, sought to live out His teachings in a world that was often hostile to their message. These early believers faced numerous challenges, from persecution to doctrinal disputes, yet they were united by a common purpose: to spread the Gospel and live in accordance with the teachings of Jesus.

Understanding the New Covenant

The New Covenant, as foretold by the prophets and established by Jesus, represents a fundamental shift from the Old Covenant. It is characterized by a direct and personal relationship with God, made possible through the life, death, and resurrection of Jesus Christ. This covenant is not based on adherence to ritualistic sacrifices, but on faith in Jesus and the transformative work of the Holy Spirit in the believer's life.

Historical Context of Traditions

The early Christians, most of whom were Israelites, initially continued to observe Hebrew customs and festivals. However, as the church grew and expanded to include Gentile believers, there was a shift in some of these practices. The apostles, guided by the Holy Spirit, began to teach that certain Hebrew rituals, such as animal sacrifice and burnt offerings, were no longer binding under the New Covenant. This shift was not always easy or smooth, leading to various debates and disagreements within the early church.

Moving Forward: A Call to Rediscovery

As we delve deeper into these topics in the chapters that follow, our goal is to rediscover the simplicity and purity of the early church's faith and practice. By examining historical developments and biblical teachings, we hope to clear away the accumulated layers of tradition that may obscure the essence of the New Covenant. This journey is not merely academic but deeply practical, calling us to align our lives more closely with the truth of the Gospel and the example of the first followers of Jesus.

Embracing the New Covenant

The journey to uncover the original intent and practice of the early church is a quest to return to the roots of the Christian faith. By examining how the first believers lived out the teachings of Jesus, we can gain valuable insights into what it means to be a follower of Christ today. This exploration will challenge us to look beyond established traditions and rediscover the transformative power of the New Covenant, inviting us to live out our faith with renewed understanding and purpose.

By peeling back the layers of historical and doctrinal developments, we aim to reveal a clearer picture of the early church's original practices and teachings. This book is an invitation to embark on a journey of rediscovery, to strip away the excess and focus on the core of our faith—the life and teachings of Jesus Christ, the foundation of the New Covenant. As we move forward, let us embrace this opportunity to grow deeper in our faith and more fully live out the calling of the Gospel.

Myth #1: Christmas Celebrates The Birth of Jesus

The nativity, now celebrated worldwide with grandeur on December 25th, was not marked by any particular festivities in the early church. This notable absence is not due to a lack of reverence for Jesus' birth but rather a focus on other aspects of His life and mission. The first followers of Christ concentrated their attention on His teachings, crucifixion, and resurrection—events that formed the bedrock of their faith and the New Covenant.

The Cultural Context of Birth Celebrations

In the cultural and religious context of the early church, the lack of emphasis on birthdays is noteworthy. Hebrew tradition did not place significant importance on the celebration of birthdays. In fact, the Bible only mentions birthdays twice, both in contexts that do not present them in a particularly positive light. The first mention is the birthday of Pharaoh, where a feast leads to the restoration of the chief cupbearer and the execution of the chief baker (Genesis 40:20-22). The second mention is the birthday of Herod, which culminates in the beheading of John the Baptist (Matthew 14:6-10, Mark 6:21-28). These accounts do not suggest a practice that the early Christians would have been eager to emulate.

Early Christian Focus: Life, Death, and Resurrection

The early Christians' primary focus was on the significant events of Jesus' ministry—His teachings, crucifixion, and resurrection. These were seen as the pivotal moments that defined the New Covenant. The birth of Jesus, while miraculous and fulfilling prophecy, was the beginning of a larger narrative that culminated in His sacrificial death and victorious resurrection. The absence of a birth celebration in the early church highlights a different set of priorities, one that emphasized the transformative power of Jesus' mission over the circumstances of His birth.

The Emergence of December 25th

The choice of December 25th as the date to celebrate Jesus' birth is rooted in historical developments that occurred centuries after the time of the early church. The selection of this date was influenced by various factors, including attempts to provide a Christian alternative to pagan festivals. December 25th coincides with the Roman festival of Saturnalia, a time of feasting and merrymaking, as well as the birthday of the unconquered sun (Sol Invictus), a celebration of the winter solstice. By aligning Jesus' birth with these dates, modern Christians sought to overlay existing pagan celebrations with their own beliefs. December 25 has never actually been shown to be the historical date of Jesus' birth.

The Influence of Pagan Traditions

The adoption of December 25th as the date for celebrating Jesus' birth reflects the broader context of the modern church's engagement with surrounding pagan cultures. The Roman Empire, within which Christianity spread, was rich with various religious traditions and festivals. As Christianity grew, there was a strategic effort to reinterpret and sanctify existing customs and practices. This approach allowed for a smoother transition for converts from paganism to Christianity but also introduced elements that were not originally part of the Christian narrative.

The Early Church's Approach to Worship

The early church's approach to worship and commemoration was markedly different from later practices. Their gatherings were simple, often taking place in homes and focused on the Communion, prayer, teaching, and fellowship. Significant attention was given to the celebration of the resurrection, which was observed at the Feast of First Fruits. This focus on the resurrection, rather than the birth of Jesus, underscores the centrality of His victory over death as the foundation of the Christian faith.

Theological Implications

Theologically, the early church's emphasis on Jesus' life, death, and resurrection over His birth can be understood in light of the New Covenant. The New Covenant, as established through Jesus' sacrificial death and resurrection, brought about a new relationship between God and humanity. This covenant was not based on lineage or birthright but on faith in Jesus Christ. Therefore, while the birth of Jesus was the necessary incarnation of God's son in human form, it was His redemptive work on the cross and His resurrection that were seen as the true transformative events.

Rediscovering the Early Church's Priorities

In rediscovering the priorities of the early church, contemporary believers can gain a deeper understanding of what it means to live out the teachings of Jesus. The early Christians' focus on the core elements of the faith—Jesus' teachings, crucifixion, and resurrection—invites modern believers to re-examine the ways in which they commemorate and celebrate their faith. It calls for a shift from ritualistic observance of modern traditions, to a profound engagement with the transformative power of the true Gospel.

Historical and Cultural Context

The birth of Jesus, as celebrated on December 25th, is a tradition that developed long after the time of the early church. The early Christians did not mark this event with any particular festivities, focusing instead on the significant events of Jesus' ministry, His death, and His resurrection. Understanding this historical and cultural context allows contemporary believers to appreciate the deeper theological significance of the New Covenant and the priorities of the early church. As we seek to uncover the original intent and practice of the early church, we are invited to align our lives more closely with the transformative message of Jesus Christ, moving beyond traditions to embrace the essence of the New Covenant.

Additional Scripture and Notes

_____

_____

_____

_____

_____

_____

_____

_____

_____

_____

_____

Myth #2: The New Moons and Sabbaths are Obsolete

The Sabbath and New Moons have always been sanctified times for God's people to meet and worship. These observances, deeply rooted in the Old Covenant, were integral to the rhythm of life and worship for the Israelites. They provided regular opportunities for reflection, repentance, and renewal. However, with the advent of the New Covenant, there was a significant shift in how these days were celebrated. The New Covenant, while not abolishing these traditions, redefined their observance in light of the transformative work of Jesus Christ.

Historical and Theological Background

Under the Old Covenant, the Sabbath was a day of rest and worship, commemorating God's rest on the seventh day of creation. The New Moon, marking the beginning of each month, was also a time for special sacrifices and offerings. These observances were commanded in the Torah and were accompanied by animal sacrifices and burnt offerings. These rituals were central to maintaining a right relationship with God and were deeply symbolic of atonement and purification.

However, these sacrifices were always intended to be temporary and symbolic. They pointed forward to a greater, ultimate sacrifice. The Apostle Paul emphasizes this by explaining that the blood of bulls and goats could never take away sins permanently (Hebrews 10:4). Instead, these sacrifices foreshadowed the coming of

Jesus, the Lamb of God, who would take away the sins of the world once and for all.

Jesus: The Fulfillment of the Sacrificial System

With the coming of Jesus, the sacrificial system of the Old Covenant was fulfilled. Jesus, as the perfect and sinless Lamb of God, offered Himself as the ultimate sacrifice for sin. His death and resurrection brought about a new reality in which the old sacrificial system was no longer necessary. The Apostle Paul, in his letters, emphasizes that the rituals and observances of the Old Covenant were shadows of the reality found in Christ (Colossians 2:16-17).

This profound theological shift had practical implications for how the early Christians observed the Sabbath and New Moons. They continued to keep these times as holy convocations, but their focus changed. The emphasis was no longer on animal sacrifices and offerings but on communion and the spiritual rest and renewal found in Christ.

Paul's Teachings on Sabbaths and New Moons

Many people refer to Apostle Paul's teachings when discussing the observance of Sabbaths and New Moons in the New Covenant. In Colossians 2:16-17, Paul writes, "Therefore do not let anyone judge you by what you eat or drink, or with regard to a religious festival, a New Moon celebration or a Sabbath day. These are a shadow of the things that were to come; the reality, however, is found in Christ."

Paul's message here is not that these observances are obsolete, but that their true meaning and significance have transitioned. The early church did not abandon the Sabbath and New Moon celebrations; rather, they reinterpreted them in light of Christ's sacrifice. The focus shifted from ritualistic adherence to the deeper spiritual truths these practices symbolized.

Hebrews 4 and the Sabbath Rest

Hebrews 4 is often cited in discussions about the Sabbath under the New Covenant. Some interpret this passage to mean that believers have a Sabbath rest in Jesus every day. However, a closer examination reveals that the Apostle Paul is specifically discussing the Sabbath day and the rest that it symbolizes. The rest spoken of in Hebrews 4 is not a generic, daily spiritual rest but a specific, eschatological rest that believers enter through faith in Jesus.

Paul makes it clear that merely keeping the Sabbath ritually is not sufficient. True Sabbath rest involves resting in the finished work of Christ. This means ceasing from our own efforts to achieve righteousness and trusting fully in His sacrifice. The Sabbath becomes a time to remember and celebrate this rest in Christ, moving beyond mere ritual to a deep, transformative experience of God's grace.

Hebrews 4 provides a profound theological insight into Christ's teaching that He is the Lord of the Sabbath (Mark 2:28). The passage speaks about entering God's rest, drawing a parallel between the rest promised to the

Israelites and the rest available to believers through faith in Jesus. Hebrews 4:9-10 states, "There remains, then, a Sabbath-rest for the people of God; for anyone who enters God's rest also rests from their works, just as God did from His." This rest is not merely about ceasing from physical labor but about entering into the spiritual rest that Jesus offers.

Communion: The New Focus of Worship

In the New Covenant, the observance of Sabbaths and New Moons shifted towards a focus on communion, the body and blood of Jesus. The early church gathered regularly to break bread and share the cup, commemorating Jesus' sacrifice and celebrating the new life found in Him. This practice, known as Communion or the Lord's Supper, became central to Christian worship.

Communion serves as a powerful reminder of Jesus' sacrifice and the New Covenant established through His blood. It is a time for believers to reflect on the profound significance of His death and resurrection, to examine their own lives, and to renew their commitment to following Him. The Sabbath and New Moons, therefore, are not abandoned but are enriched by this new focus on communion.

Observance of the Sabbath by Jesus, Paul, and the Disciples

Despite the transformative shift in how the Sabbath and New Moons were observed, it is evident from the New

Testament that Jesus, the Apostle Paul, and all of the disciples continued to honor these sacred times. Jesus Himself observed the Sabbath throughout His ministry. The Gospels record numerous instances where Jesus attended synagogue services on the Sabbath, taught the people, and healed the sick. For example, in Luke 4:16, it is noted, "He went to Nazareth, where he had been brought up, and on the Sabbath day he went into the synagogue, as was his custom." This clearly shows that Jesus maintained the Sabbath observance, though He also redefined its meaning by emphasizing acts of mercy and goodness over strict legalistic adherence.

Similarly, the Apostle Paul and the early disciples continued to observe the Sabbath. Acts 17:2 recounts, "As was his custom, Paul went into the synagogue, and on three Sabbath days he reasoned with them from the Scriptures." This passage illustrates that Paul regularly attended synagogue services on the Sabbath, using the opportunity to teach about Jesus and the New Covenant. Furthermore, Acts 18:4 states, "Every Sabbath he reasoned in the synagogue, trying to persuade Jews and Greeks." These references indicate that Paul and the early Christian community did not abandon the Sabbath; rather, they used it as a time for gathering, teaching, and spreading the Gospel.

The Sabbath in the Early Christian Community

The continued observance of the Sabbath by Jesus, Paul, and the disciples highlights the importance of this day within the early Christian community. They upheld the Sabbath as a day of worship, teaching, and fellowship, but with a renewed focus on the message and mission of Jesus Christ. The early church understood the Sabbath not merely as a day of physical rest but as a profound symbol of the spiritual rest and renewal found in Christ. This observance was not marked by the old practices of animal sacrifices but by a deeper engagement with the teachings of Jesus and the celebration of His resurrection.

The Continuation of Sacred Times

The transition of the New Moon and Sabbath observances under the New Covenant does not negate their sanctity. Instead, it reorients their purpose. The early Christians understood that these times were still holy, but their celebration was transformed. No longer centered on animal sacrifices, these days became opportunities to gather as a community, to worship, to pray, and to partake in the Lord's Supper.

This continuity and transformation highlight the depth and richness of the New Covenant. It honors the sacred traditions of the past while revealing their ultimate fulfillment in Jesus. By understanding this, modern believers can appreciate the significance of these observances and celebrate them in a way that honors Christ's sacrifice and the new life it brings.

Additional Scripture and Notes

_____

_____

_____

_____

_____

_____

_____

_____

_____

_____

_____

Myth #3: Easter Celebrates Christ's Resurrection

Easter is one of the most widely celebrated holidays in Christianity, commemorating the resurrection of Jesus Christ. However, the name "Easter" and some of its associated traditions have roots in pagan festivals, leading to questions about its historical and theological connections to the events of Jesus' sacrifice and resurrection. In contrast, Passover, a significant Israelite festival, is closely tied to these pivotal moments in the Christian faith. Understanding the origins and meanings of Easter and Passover can help believers appreciate the profound significance of Jesus' sacrifice and resurrection and consider how best to commemorate these events.

Pagan Roots of Easter

The name "Easter" is derived from "Eostre," a pagan goddess associated with spring and fertility. Many customs traditionally associated with Easter, such as eggs and rabbits, have origins in pre-Christian, pagan spring celebrations. These symbols represented new life and rebirth, aligning with the theme of resurrection but lacking direct ties to the biblical narrative of Jesus' death and resurrection.

Historically, the early church did not celebrate Easter as it is known today. The observance of Jesus' resurrection was originally integrated into the Hebrew Passover celebration. The Council of Nicaea in 325 AD, however, established a separate date for Easter, aligning it with the spring equinox and distancing it from Passover. This separation introduced various pagan elements into the celebration, leading to the hybrid holiday observed today.

The term "Easter" appears only once in the King James Version of the Bible, in Acts 12:4. However, this is widely recognized as a mistranslation. The original Greek word used in this verse is "Pascha," which means Passover. The mistranslation to "Easter" has led to confusion, as Easter, with its pagan origins and associations with the goddess Eostre, has little to do with the Hebrew festival of Passover.

Biblical Foundations of Passover

Passover has deep biblical roots and is intrinsically linked to the story of Jesus' sacrifice. The Passover festival commemorates the Israelites' deliverance from slavery in Egypt, as described in the book of Exodus. During the Passover meal, a lamb was sacrificed, and its blood marked the doorposts of the Israelites' homes, sparing them from the final plague. This lamb, known as the Passover lamb, prefigures Jesus Christ, who is often referred to as the Lamb of God.

The Apostle Paul explicitly makes this connection in 1 Corinthians 5:7, stating, "For Christ, our Passover lamb, has been sacrificed." Jesus' crucifixion occurred during the Passover festival, and His Last Supper with His disciples was a Passover meal. This timing is not coincidental; it underscores the fulfillment of the Passover symbolism in Jesus' sacrificial death.

The Feast of Unleavened Bread and First Fruits

Following Passover, the Feast of Unleavened Bread and the Feast of First Fruits hold additional significance in the context of Jesus' death and resurrection. The Feast of Unleavened Bread, lasting seven days, begins immediately after Passover. Leaven, symbolizing sin and corruption, is removed from homes, paralleling the sinless sacrifice of Jesus. As Paul notes in 1 Corinthians 5:8, believers are to celebrate "the festival, not with the old leaven, the leaven of malice and evil, but with the unleavened bread of sincerity and truth."

The Feast of First Fruits occurs on the day after the Sabbath following Passover, marking the beginning of the barley harvest. Biblically, it signifies offering the first portion of the harvest to God in thanksgiving. In Christian theology, Jesus' resurrection is seen as the fulfillment of First Fruits. Paul refers to Jesus as "the firstfruits of those who have fallen asleep" (1 Corinthians 15:20), indicating that His resurrection is the first of the new, eternal life promised to believers.

Theological Implications

The close alignment of Jesus' death and resurrection with the Israelite festivals of Passover, Unleavened Bread, and First Fruits provides rich theological symbolism. Jesus is the true Passover Lamb, whose sacrifice brings deliverance from sin and death. His sinless life is symbolized by the unleavened bread, and His resurrection is the firstfruits of the new creation.

These connections deepen the understanding of Jesus' mission and the significance of His work.

Celebrating Passover as Christians

Given the profound biblical connections, Christians in the New Covenant are directed to observe Passover and the related feasts as a way to honor Jesus' life, death, and resurrection. This observance can provide a richer, more biblically grounded experience of the events central to the Christian faith. Celebrating Passover involves participating in a Passover meal, recounting the Exodus story, and reflecting on its fulfillment in Jesus. The Feast of Unleavened Bread can be a time for spiritual reflection and cleansing, removing the "leaven" of sin from one's life. The Feast of First Fruits can be celebrated by acknowledging Jesus' resurrection and offering gratitude for the new life it brings.

Historical Truth

Easter, with its pagan roots and later historical developments, stands in contrast to the biblically grounded festivals of Passover, Unleavened Bread, and First Fruits. Understanding these origins and their theological significance invites believers to consider how they commemorate Jesus' sacrifice and resurrection. Embracing these high holy days offers a way to honor Jesus' life, death, and resurrection in a manner that is rich in biblical symbolism and rooted in the historical context of His sacrifice.

Additional Scripture and Notes

Myth #4: Denominations are a Part of Christianity

One of the most significant challenges facing the church today is the proliferation of denominations. These divisions often arise from differing interpretations of Scripture and practice, leading to fragmented communities that sometimes view each other with suspicion or even hostility. Yet, Jesus' prayer for His followers was that they would be one, as He and the Father are one (John 17:21). This vision of unity stands in stark contrast to the reality of denominational divisions that characterize much of contemporary Christianity.

The Early Church and the Call for Unity

The early church experienced its own struggles with unity, as evidenced by the Apostle Paul's letters. In 1 Corinthians 1:10-13, Paul addresses the issue of divisions within the Corinthian church, urging the believers to be "perfectly united in mind and thought." He reproves them for aligning themselves with different leaders—Paul, Apollos, Cephas, or Christ—stating that such divisions are detrimental to the body of Christ. Paul emphasizes that Christ is not divided and that believers should not be either.

The early church was not free from doctrinal disputes or differing practices, but it was fundamentally united by a common faith in Jesus Christ and a commitment to the core message of the Gospel. This unity was not about uniformity in all things but about a shared allegiance to

Jesus as Lord and a communal commitment to living out His teachings. The church was seen as the body of believers, encompassing Israelites and Gentiles alike, with Christ as the head. There were no denominations like Baptist, Pentecostal, Seventh Day Adventist, Mormons, Jehovah's Witness, Israel United in Christ, ISUPK, or various other groups that exist today. The early Christians were simply known as followers of "The Way" (Acts 9:2), united in their faith and mission.

The Rise of Denominations

Over time, as Christianity spread and developed, differing interpretations of Scripture and theological nuances led to the formation of distinct groups. These groups often solidified into denominations, each with its own set of beliefs, practices, and governance structures. While some differences were relatively minor, others were significant enough to create lasting divisions.

The Reformation in the 16th century marked a major turning point, as reformers like Martin Luther, John Calvin, and others broke away from the Roman Catholic Church to form new Protestant denominations. These movements were driven by a desire to return to what they saw as the true teachings of Scripture and to correct perceived errors and corruptions in the established church. While the Reformation was instrumental in bringing about necessary changes and revitalizing Christian faith for many, it also led to the fragmentation of the church into numerous denominations.

The Challenge of Denominationalism

Denominationalism presents a significant challenge to the unity of the church. Each denomination often emphasizes its own interpretations and traditions, sometimes to the detriment of fostering a broader sense of Christian unity. These divisions can lead to a lack of cooperation, mutual suspicion, and even outright hostility among believers. The church's witness to the world can be compromised when it appears divided and conflicted.

Furthermore, denominationalism can create barriers to fellowship and collaboration. Believers may find it difficult to worship together, serve together, or even recognize each other as part of the same body of Christ. This fragmentation is contrary to Jesus' prayer for unity and the early church's example of a diverse yet united community of faith.

The Call to Unity

Despite these challenges, the call to unity remains a central and enduring aspect of Christian life. Achieving true unity requires humility, mutual respect, and a focus on the core message of the Gospel. It involves recognizing that, while there are important theological differences, these should not overshadow the shared foundation of faith in Jesus Christ.

Paul's letters are filled with exhortations to maintain unity. In Ephesians 4:3-6, he urges believers to "make every effort to keep the unity of the Spirit through the bond of peace. There is one body and one Spirit, just as you were called to one hope when you were called; one Lord, one faith, one baptism; one God and Father of all, who is over all and through all and in all." This passage highlights the fundamental oneness that should characterize the church, grounded in the shared confession of faith and the work of the Holy Spirit.

Moving Toward Unity

Moving toward greater unity involves several key principles. First, it requires a commitment to the authority of Scripture and a willingness to engage in open, respectful dialogue about differing interpretations. Believers must prioritize the core truths of the faith—such as the divinity of Christ, His resurrection, and the call to love and serve others—while allowing for diversity in non-essential matters.

Second, unity requires a spirit of humility and repentance. The Christ Faithful must be willing to acknowledge their own biases and shortcomings, seeking forgiveness and reconciliation where there has been division and strife. This includes a readiness to listen to and learn from one another, recognizing that no single tradition has a monopoly on truth.

Third, unity involves practical steps toward collaboration and fellowship. This can include joint worship services, community service projects, and theological forums where believers from different denominations come together to explore common ground and work toward shared goals. By focusing on what unites rather than what divides, the church can present a more unified witness to the world.

The Church as One Body

Ultimately, the church is called to be one body, with Christ as the head. This vision of unity transcends denominational labels and focuses on the essential identity of the church as the people of God. In 1 Corinthians 12:12-13, Paul writes, "Just as a body, though one, has many parts, but all its many parts form one body, so it is with Christ. For we were all baptized by one Spirit so as to form one body—whether Israelites or Gentiles, slave or free—and we were all given the one Spirit to drink."

By embracing this vision, believers can work toward a more united and effective church, one that reflects the love, grace, and truth of Jesus Christ. The call to unity is not merely a lofty ideal but a practical imperative for the church today. It requires dedication, perseverance, and a willingness to place the mission of the Gospel above individual or denominational preferences.

Additional Scripture and Notes

_____

_____

_____

_____

_____

_____

_____

_____

_____

_____

_____

Myth #5: Believers Must Attend Church Sunday Mornings

The Bible does not explicitly command believers to worship in a dedicated building on Sunday mornings. Instead, the early church gathered in homes, public spaces, and wherever believers could meet to share in fellowship and worship. This practice underscores the biblical understanding that the true church is the collective body of believers, not a physical structure. The emphasis in the New Testament is on communal worship, prayer, and the breaking of bread, regardless of location. While gathering on Sundays became a tradition to honor Christ's resurrection, it is not mandated as the sole or required day of worship. Instead, believers are encouraged to worship God continually and to observe the biblically prescribed times of convocation, such as the Sabbaths, New Moons, and Holy Days. Again, it is fine to worship on Sunday mornings, but it must be realized that this is not a biblically mandated time to worship. Believers should not be judged for not attending Sunday morning service.

The Church as a Living Community

In the early days of Christianity, the concept of the church was centered on the people, not a physical structure. Believers gathered in homes, public spaces, and sometimes in temples. This practice is well-documented in the New Testament. For instance, in Acts 2:46, we read, "Every day they continued to meet together in the temple courts. They broke bread in their homes and ate together with glad and sincere hearts."

These gatherings were marked by communal worship, teaching, fellowship, and the breaking of bread, reflecting a vibrant, interconnected community.

The Apostle Paul, in his letters, frequently addressed the church as the collective body of believers rather than a specific location. In 1 Corinthians 12:27, he writes, "Now you are the body of Christ, and each one of you is a part of it." This imagery emphasizes that the church's essence lies in its people—each member contributing to the whole, united by their faith in Jesus Christ.

The Institutionalization of the Church

The institutionalization of the church and the construction of dedicated buildings came much later. As Christianity became more established, especially after Constantine's Edict of Milan in 313 AD, which legalized Christian worship, the faith transitioned from a persecuted sect to an accepted, and eventually dominant, religion. This shift led to the construction of basilicas and church buildings, which played a significant role in the public and communal life of Christians.

While these developments helped Christianity to flourish and become more organized, they also introduced a tendency to equate the church with its buildings. The focus often shifted from the people and their communal worship to the place where they gathered. This perspective can lead to a reductionist view where attending a building on Sunday is seen as the primary expression of being a Christian.

Reclaiming the Early Church's Understanding

Reclaiming the early church's understanding involves recognizing that the true church is not confined to walls but is a global, diverse body of believers. The church is defined by the people who comprise it and their collective commitment to follow Jesus. This means that the church exists wherever believers are gathered—in homes, workplaces, schools, and public spaces. This perspective invites a more dynamic and inclusive view of what it means to be the church.

Sunday Worship and Biblical Commandments

Another area where tradition has diverged from the early church's practices is the observance of Sunday worship. Many people today define Christianity as those who go to a church building on Sunday mornings. While gathering on Sunday to celebrate the resurrection of Christ is a longstanding tradition, it is not a biblical commandment. The New Covenant does not mandate Sunday as the sole day of worship.

The practice of meeting on Sunday, the first day of the week, emerged because it was the day Jesus rose from the dead. Acts 20:7 mentions, "On the first day of the week we came together to break bread," indicating that early Christians did gather on Sundays. However, this practice was not instituted as a replacement for the

Sabbath but as an additional time of fellowship and worship.

The actual mandated times for convocation according to the Bible are Sabbaths, New Moons, and High Holy days. The Sabbath, observed from Friday evening to Saturday evening, was never changed to Sunday in the early church. Some early Christians did meet on Sundays to honor the risen Christ, but this did not supplant the Sabbath. Hebrews 4:9-10 reiterates the importance of the Sabbath rest, pointing to a deeper, spiritual rest in Christ.

The Church in Name and Practice

Another aspect of the modern misconception is the naming and organizational structures of churches today. Names like First Baptist Church, Mount Zion Missionary, St. Mary's, and Calvary Chapel reflect a denominational and institutional approach that differs from the early church. In the New Testament, the church was simply called the church, distinguished only by its location, such as the church in Ephesus, Sardis, or Philadelphia.

This naming convention underscores that the church is not a building or an institution but the people who comprise it. The early Christians understood their identity as part of the universal body of Christ, transcending geographical and cultural boundaries. This understanding fostered a sense of unity and shared mission that is sometimes lacking in modern denominational contexts.

Additional Scripture and Notes

Myth #6: Financial Tithing is an Obligation

Tithing, a practice deeply rooted in the Old Testament, was transformed in the early church from a rigid requirement to an expression of voluntary generosity. This evolution reflects a broader movement under the New Covenant from the letter of the law to the spirit of the law. Understanding this shift is crucial for contemporary Christians seeking to align their financial practices with biblical principles.

The Old Testament Practice of Tithing

In the Old Testament, tithing was a well-defined practice. The Israelites were commanded to give a tenth of their produce and livestock, to the Levites. The Levites did not have their own land and depended on these tithes for their sustenance (Numbers 18:21-24). This system ensured that the spiritual leaders were supported and that the temple and its services were maintained.

The tithe was primarily agricultural, consisting of grain, fruit, and livestock. It was not a monetary contribution intended to accumulate wealth for the Levites or their families but a practical provision for those who dedicated their lives to serving God and the community. The purpose of tithing was to ensure fairness and support for those without inheritance in the land, highlighting a communal approach to resource management.

The New Testament Shift: Generosity Over Obligation

With the advent of the New Covenant, the early church's approach to giving underwent a significant transformation. The ten percent mandate of the Old Testament was replaced by a focus on generosity and voluntary giving. The Apostle Paul encapsulates this shift in 2 Corinthians 9:7, where he writes, "Each of you should give what you have decided in your heart to give, not reluctantly or under compulsion, for God loves a cheerful giver."

This emphasis on cheerful and willing giving highlights a critical distinction: the heart's posture is more important than the percentage given. The early Christians were encouraged to give according to their means and in response to the needs of the community. This practice underscored a broader principle of financial stewardship that went beyond mere compliance with a set percentage.

Holistic Stewardship and Sacrificial Giving

The shift from tithing as an obligation to a model of generous giving reflects the New Covenant's emphasis on holistic stewardship and sacrificial giving. Jesus taught that true generosity involves giving sacrificially, as exemplified by the widow who gave two small coins but was praised for giving all she had (Mark 12:41-44). This teaching moves believers from a transactional view of tithing to a relational and sacrificial approach to financial stewardship.

In the New Testament, the focus on caring for the poor and needy is much more pronounced than the specific act of tithing. James 1:27 defines pure and faultless religion as looking after orphans and widows in their distress, and Acts 2:44-45 describes the early believers selling their possessions and goods to give to anyone who had need. This radical generosity and communal sharing were central to the life of the early church.

Misconceptions and Modern Practices

Despite the New Testament's emphasis on voluntary and cheerful giving, the practice of tithing as a defined percentage has persisted in many Christian traditions. This persistence sometimes overshadows the broader call to holistic stewardship and sacrificial giving. Some pastors and church leaders teach that failing to tithe is equivalent to robbing God, referencing Malachi 3:8-10. However, this Old Testament passage must be understood in its historical and covenantal context, which differs from the principles of giving laid out in the New Testament.

The practice of tithing in contemporary churches often includes financial contributions to support church operations, pastoral salaries, and community outreach. While supporting the church and its ministries is essential, it should not be framed as a divine mandate that equates to tithing under the Old Covenant. Instead, it should be presented as an opportunity for believers to contribute to the collective mission and needs of the church body.

Reclaiming Biblical Stewardship

Reclaiming the early church's understanding of financial stewardship involves several key principles:

1. **Voluntary Generosity**: Giving should be voluntary and motivated by love and compassion, not by a sense of obligation or guilt. Believers are called to give cheerfully and according to their means, as Paul instructed.
2. **Sacrificial Giving**: True generosity often involves sacrifice. Christians are encouraged to give in a way that reflects their commitment to Christ and the needs of the community, following the example of the early believers.
3. **Holistic Stewardship**: Financial stewardship encompasses more than just giving to the church. It involves managing all resources—time, talents, and finances—in a way that honors God and serves others. This includes caring for the poor, supporting missions, and contributing to the welfare of the community.
4. **Community Focus**: The early church's communal approach to resource management highlights the importance of supporting one another. Believers are called to be attentive to the needs within their community and to respond with generosity and compassion.
5. **Educational Approach**: Church leaders should educate their congregations on the principles of New Testament giving, emphasizing voluntary generosity, holistic stewardship, and sacrificial giving. This education can help shift the focus

from a rigid tithing mandate to a more comprehensive and biblically aligned approach to financial stewardship.

Prosperity Gospel

A common misconception is the belief that the more one tithes, the more one will receive in return. This "prosperity gospel" notion misrepresents biblical teaching. The Bible does not promise material wealth as a direct result of tithing. Instead, giving should be done responsibly and according to one's means, not with the expectation of financial gain. Paul emphasizes that the true blessing comes from giving willingly and cheerfully, rather than from a transactional or "lottery" mindset that expects a return of wealth and blessings for contributions made to an organization.

Additional Scripture and Notes

_____

_____

_____

_____

_____

_____

_____

_____

_____

_____

_____

Myth #7: The Dietary Laws Are Done Away With

The question of dietary laws stands as a testament to the early church's journey in defining its identity amidst a shifting landscape of traditions and teachings. Jesus Christ's words in Mark 7:19, declaring that it is not food that makes one unclean but the heart, have often been misconstrued as an abolishment of his Father's laws. However, Jesus himself clarified his stance: "Think not that I am come to destroy the law, or the prophets: I am not come to destroy, but to fulfil." This statement underscores Jesus's adherence to the divine laws laid out in the Old Testament, including the dietary laws.

The Purpose and Continuity of Dietary Laws

In the Old Testament, God established dietary laws for the Israelites, delineating clean and unclean animals (Leviticus 11). These laws were not arbitrary but served a dual purpose: to maintain physical health and to symbolize spiritual purity and separation from the nations around them. The prohibition against consuming certain animals like pork, shellfish, and scavengers was rooted in God's desire for his people to live holy lives, set apart for his purposes.

Jesus's teaching in Mark 7 challenged the superficial understanding of cleanliness based solely on external rituals. He emphasized that true purity begins within the heart, highlighting the spiritual intent behind the dietary laws. His teachings did not negate the validity of the laws themselves but emphasized their deeper spiritual significance.

Paul and the New Covenant Perspective

The Apostle Paul's writings further illuminate the relationship between the Old Testament laws and the New Covenant established through Jesus Christ. Paul acknowledges that the law acted as a "schoolmaster" or guardian, guiding Israel until the coming of Christ (Galatians 3:24-25). While the sacrificial and ceremonial aspects of the law were fulfilled in Christ's atoning sacrifice, the moral and ethical principles, including those regarding diet, remain relevant.

Paul's teachings in Romans 3:31 affirm, "Do we then make void the law through faith? God forbid: yea, we establish the law." This statement underscores the continuity and enduring relevance of God's laws, including dietary guidelines, in the life of a believer under the New Covenant.

Health and Holiness: A Biblical Perspective

The dietary laws were not only about spiritual purity but also about physical health. Many of the foods prohibited under the Old Testament laws, such as pork and shellfish, are known today to carry health risks such as parasites and toxins. Modern medical research confirms that adhering to these dietary principles can contribute to better health outcomes, reducing risks of heart disease, obesity, high blood pressure, diabetes, and certain cancers.

The Bible teaches that our bodies are temples of the Holy Spirit (1 Corinthians 6:19), emphasizing the importance of stewardship over our physical well-being. By adhering to God's dietary laws, believers honor their bodies as sacred vessels, worthy of respect and care. Eating a balanced diet that includes a variety of fruits, vegetables, and clean meats aligns with biblical principles of health and holiness.

Consistency in God's Character and Law

God's character is unchanging, and his moral principles are eternal. The same God who declared certain foods unclean in the Old Testament does not alter his standards in the New Testament. Malachi 3:6 declares, "I the Lord do not change." Therefore, the notion that God would suddenly declare previously forbidden foods as acceptable contradicts the biblical understanding of God's consistency and holiness.

Additional Scripture and Notes

_____

_____

_____

_____

_____

_____

_____

_____

_____

_____

_____

Myth #8: It's Ok to Celebrate Pagan Holidays

Celebrating pagan holidays often involves traditions and practices that are rooted in idolatry and contrary to biblical teachings. These holidays can detract from the spiritual significance of the biblical High Holy Days, which God instituted as perpetual observances for His people (Perpetual means never ending or changing). The Bible warns against following the ways of pagans and the traditions of men, urging believers to keep the holy days commanded by God instead. By celebrating the biblical High Holy Days—such as Passover, Unleavened Bread, First Fruits, Pentecost, Trumpets, Atonement, and Tabernacles—believers honor God's commands, remember His mighty works, and align their worship with His ordained calendar. These celebrations help maintain the purity of faith and draw believers closer to the divine truths embedded in these sacred observances.

Biblical Foundation of High Holy Days

In the Old Testament, God instituted seven High Holy days as part of Israel's religious calendar: Passover, Unleavened Bread, First Fruits, Pentecost (Feast of Weeks), Blowing of Trumpets, Atonement (Yom Kippur), and Tabernacles (Sukkot). These festivals were not merely cultural traditions but divine appointments designed to commemorate significant events in Israel's history and foreshadow future spiritual realities.

Jesus, Paul, and the Apostolic Tradition

Jesus Christ and his disciples faithfully observed these High Holy days throughout their lives. Jesus's crucifixion during the Feast of Passover and his resurrection during the Feast of First Fruits underscore the fulfillment of these festivals in his life and ministry. The Apostle Paul continued this tradition, often planning his journeys to coincide with these appointed times (Acts 20:16).

Paul's teachings emphasize the spiritual significance of these festivals in revealing God's redemptive plan through Jesus Christ. For instance, Pentecost, originally a harvest festival when the Torah was given, became the day when the Holy Spirit was poured out on the early church, marking the beginning of the New Covenant era (Acts 2).

Contrast with Pagan Traditions

In contrast to the divine origin and perpetual nature of the High Holy days, modern society has embraced numerous pagan customs and traditions. Holidays like Halloween, Valentine's Day, Thanksgiving, and New Year's Eve often incorporate elements with pagan origins or practices that diverge from biblical principles.

The Bible explicitly warns against adopting the practices of pagan nations and emphasizes the importance of adhering to God's ordained traditions. Deuteronomy 12:30-31 cautions, "Take heed to yourself that you are not ensnared to follow them...for every abomination to the Lord which He hates they have done to their gods."

Forsaking Gluttony

The High Holy Day feasts prescribed in the Bible are not about gluttony and materialism but rather about reverence, reflection, and community. Unlike many pagan holidays that often emphasize excessive consumption and material indulgence, the biblical feasts feature modest amounts of food and are centered on spiritual significance. These holy days are times for believers to come together in worship and remembrance, with fasting also being an integral part of traditional practices. For instance, the Day of Atonement involves a full 24-hour fast, emphasizing repentance and humility before God. This contrast highlights the sacred purpose of the High Holy Days, which is to honor God and deepen spiritual commitment, rather than indulge in excess.

Reclaiming God's Ordained Festivals

As believers in Jesus Christ, reclaiming and celebrating the High Holy days reclaiming and celebrating the New Covenant's understanding of these festivals is an opportunity to honor God's commands and deepen our understanding of His redemptive plan. These appointed times serve as reminders of God's faithfulness, His deliverance, and His ongoing work in our lives and in the world.

Embracing Biblical Festivals Today

Today, there is a growing movement among Christians to rediscover and celebrate the biblical High Holy days in their original context. This includes Passover, where believers reflect on Christ's sacrifice as the true Passover Lamb; Unleavened Bread, symbolizing the removal of sin from our lives; First Fruits, celebrating Christ's resurrection; Pentecost, commemorating the outpouring of the Holy Spirit; Trumpets, looking forward to Christ's return; Atonement, reflecting on reconciliation with God through Christ's atoning sacrifice; and Tabernacles, recalling God's provision and presence among His people.

Additional Information

The High Holy days ordained by God are not outdated rituals but enduring reminders of His faithfulness, His redemptive plan through Jesus Christ, and His desire for His people to remember and celebrate His appointed times. By embracing these biblical festivals and rejecting pagan customs, believers can honor God's commands, deepen their faith, and bear witness to God's work in the world. For further guidance on observing these sacred days, resources published by Blackstone Publishing such as "Bible Approved Holidays: Ending Pagan Rituals", "New Moon Communion Journal", and "The Holy Sabbath: A Covenant for God's People" provide practical insights and reflections for celebrating these significant occasions in alignment with biblical truth. Find them at www.bspbooks.com.

Additional Scripture and Notes

_____

_____

_____

_____

_____

_____

_____

_____

_____

_____

_____

Myth #9: Eternity Begins with the Afterlife

Many Christians today live with their eyes fixed on the promise of heaven, often overlooking the significance of their lives on earth. While the hope of eternal life with God is a central tenet of the Christian faith, it is equally important to understand that Jesus called us to live out the values of heaven here and now. The prayer "Thy kingdom come, Thy will be done on earth as it is in heaven" (Matthew 6:10) underscores the belief that our earthly existence should reflect heavenly realities.

Living Eternity Now

Eternity is not a distant future but a present reality that begins now. Eternity is defined as infinite or unending time. It encompasses the concept of existence without beginning or end, transcending the temporal and finite nature of human experience. This definition confirms that eternity does not begin at a future date but includes the now.

By embracing the values of God's kingdom in our finances, health, relationships, and obedience to His laws, we can experience a foretaste of heaven on earth. Living out "on earth as it is in heaven" means embodying the wholeness, peace, and justice of God's kingdom in our daily lives. As we repent and align ourselves with God's will, we become agents of His kingdom, bringing the realities of heaven into our present world.

The Misconception of Earthly Suffering

A prevalent misconception among many believers is the idea that life on earth is meant to be a period of suffering and hardship, with relief and joy reserved solely for heaven. This perspective often leads to a passive acceptance of poverty, sickness, and struggle, with the hope that everything will be rectified in the afterlife. While it is true that trials and tribulations are part of the human experience, the Bible also teaches that God's kingdom can and should be experienced here on earth.

Living Out Heaven's Values on Earth

Jesus's ministry emphasized the importance of living out the principles of God's kingdom in our daily lives. When He declared, "The kingdom of heaven is at hand" (Matthew 4:17), He was announcing that the values and realities of heaven were breaking into the present world. This proclamation calls for a transformative way of living that reflects the wholeness, peace, and justice of God's reign.

Financial Stewardship and Prosperity

One area where many Christians struggle is in their financial lives. The Bible does not advocate for a life of poverty but rather teaches principles of good stewardship, generosity, and responsible financial planning. Proverbs 21:20 says, "There is treasure to be desired and oil in the dwelling of the wise; but a foolish man spendeth it up." This verse highlights the importance of managing resources wisely.

Furthermore, 3 John 1:2 expresses God's desire for His people to prosper: "Beloved, I wish above all things that thou mayest prosper and be in health, even as thy soul prospereth." Financial stability and prosperity are part of living a life that honors God, enabling believers to provide for their families, support their communities, and contribute to the work of the kingdom.

Health and Wellness

Health is another critical aspect of experiencing God's kingdom on earth. While physical ailments and diseases are part of the fallen world, the Bible encourages us to seek health and healing. Isaiah 53:5 tells us, "By his stripes we are healed," pointing to the holistic healing that comes through Christ's sacrifice. Believers are called to be good stewards of their bodies, recognizing them as temples of the Holy Spirit (1 Corinthians 6:19).

A balanced diet, regular exercise, and adequate rest are practical ways to honor God with our bodies. The Bible provides guidelines for healthy living, including dietary laws that promote well-being. By taking care of our physical health, we reflect the wholeness of God's kingdom in our lives.

Relationships and Community

Strong, healthy relationships are a cornerstone of living out heaven's values on earth. Jesus emphasized the importance of love, forgiveness, and reconciliation in our interactions with others. John 13:34-35 records Jesus's commandment to love one another: "A new commandment I give unto you, That ye love one another; as I have loved you, that ye also love one another. By this shall all men know that ye are my disciples, if ye have love one to another."

Building and maintaining healthy relationships requires effort, communication, and a willingness to forgive. It also involves being part of a community of believers who support and encourage one another in their faith journeys. The early church modeled this community life, sharing their resources and caring for each other's needs (Acts 2:44-47).

Repentance and Obedience

The key to experiencing heaven on earth lies in repentance and obedience to God's laws. Repentance involves turning away from sin and aligning our lives with God's will. Jesus's call to "Repent: for the kingdom of heaven is at hand" (Matthew 4:17) is a call to transform our hearts and lives to reflect God's kingdom.

Obedience to God's commandments, including the moral and ethical teachings of the Bible, is essential for living out the values of heaven. While the sacrificial laws were fulfilled in Christ, the rest of the laws remain a guide for righteous living. Jesus affirmed the importance of the law in Matthew 5:17: "Think not that I am come to destroy the law, or the prophets: I am not come to destroy, but to fulfil."

The Nature of Sin and God's Law

Understanding sin is crucial to living out the values of God's kingdom on earth. The Bible explicitly defines sin as the breaking of God's law. 1 John 3:4 states, "Whosoever committeth sin transgresseth also the law: for sin is the transgression of the law." This verse underscores that sin is not merely a moral failing or a mistake but a direct violation of God's commandments. Recognizing this helps us understand the gravity of sin and the importance of repentance. It also highlights the need for believers to adhere to God's laws, as these laws provide the framework for righteous living. By aligning our lives with God's commandments, we can avoid sin and live in a way that honors Him, bringing the principles of heaven into our daily existence.

Additional Scripture and Notes

Myth #10: God is Outside of Us

The External Focus on God

Many believers today tend to focus on God as an external force, seeking divine intervention in their lives while overlooking the profound presence of God within them. This external focus often leads to a passive approach to faith, where individuals wait for God to act rather than recognizing the power of the Holy Spirit residing within them. They also tend to externalize the concept of evil, attributing their failings to an external devil rather than taking responsibility for their actions and choices. Understanding the Kingdom of God as an internal reality can transform how we live our faith, emphasizing personal accountability and the active presence of God within us.

The Indwelling of the Holy Spirit

When Jesus spoke of the Kingdom of God, He emphasized its internal nature. In Luke 17:21, He said, "Neither shall they say, Lo here! or, lo there! for, behold, the kingdom of God is within you." This profound statement highlights that God's kingdom is not confined to a specific place but is a dynamic, spiritual reality within each believer. The Holy Spirit, given to us through faith in Christ, is the embodiment of this internal kingdom. The Spirit's presence within us guides, empowers, and leads us into all truth, making the divine accessible in our daily lives.

Personal Accountability and Transformation

Acknowledging the Kingdom of God within us requires a shift from blaming external forces to taking personal accountability for our actions. Many of our failings and struggles arise from our own decisions and behaviors, rather than from an external devil. James 1:14-15 explains, "But every man is tempted, when he is drawn away of his own lust, and enticed. Then when lust hath conceived, it bringeth forth sin: and sin, when it is finished, bringeth forth death." Recognizing our role in our struggles is the first step towards transformation and growth.

The Power of the Holy Spirit

The Holy Spirit within us is a powerful source of guidance, comfort, and truth. Jesus promised in John 14:26, "But the Comforter, which is the Holy Spirit, whom the Father will send in my name, he shall teach you all things, and bring all things to your remembrance, whatsoever I have said unto you." This promise assures us that we have access to divine wisdom and guidance directly through the Spirit's indwelling presence. By cultivating a deeper relationship with the Holy Spirit, we can navigate life's challenges with divine insight and strength.

Moving Beyond Dependence on External Authorities

While seeking counsel from godly people and pastors is valuable, it is crucial to balance this with a personal relationship with God. The apostle John reminds us in 1 John 2:27, "But the anointing which ye have received of him abideth in you, and ye need not that any man teach you: but as the same anointing teacheth you of all things, and is truth, and is no lie, and even as it hath taught you, ye shall abide in him." This verse emphasizes the sufficiency of the Holy Spirit's teaching within us, encouraging us to rely on God's internal guidance alongside external support.

Practical Steps to Tap into the God Within

1. **Regular Prayer and Meditation:** Spend time in quiet reflection and conversation with God, inviting the Holy Spirit to speak and guide you.
2. **Study the Scriptures:** Engage with the Bible not just as a historical document but as a living word that the Holy Spirit can illuminate and apply to your life.
3. **Practice Self-Examination:** Regularly assess your actions and motives, seeking to align them with God's will and taking responsibility for your choices.
4. **Cultivate Spiritual Disciplines:** Fasting, worship, and other spiritual practices can help you become more attuned to the Holy Spirit's presence and leading.
5. **Seek Community Support:** While emphasizing personal accountability, also engage with a community of believers who can offer support, encouragement, and accountability.

The Internal Reality

Understanding that the Kingdom of God is within us transforms our approach to faith and life. It shifts our focus from external forces to the internal reality of the Holy Spirit's presence and power. This understanding calls us to personal accountability, recognizing that many of our struggles are self-inflicted and can be overcome through the guidance of the Holy Spirit. By tapping into the God within us, we can experience a deeper, more transformative faith that empowers us to live out the values of God's kingdom in our daily lives.

Additional Scripture and Notes

_____

_____

_____

_____

_____

_____

_____

_____

_____

_____

_____

_____

Heavenly Father,

Thank you for the truth of the New Covenant, sealed by the precious blood of Jesus Christ. We praise you for your faithfulness throughout generations, guiding us with your unfailing love and grace.

Lord, in this covenant, you have shown us your mercy and forgiveness, lifting the burden of our sins through Christ's sacrifice. We stand redeemed and reconciled to you, no longer blinded by myth but liberated by your truth.

Father, help us to live in the fullness of this truth each day. May we walk in the light of your Word, guided by the Holy Spirit who dwells within us. Grant us wisdom and discernment to understand your will and the courage to obey it.

As we embrace the freedom and love of the New Covenant, may our lives reflect your glory. Help us to love others as you have loved us, showing compassion, grace, and forgiveness to those around us.

Lord, we thank you for the promise of eternal life through Jesus Christ. May our hearts overflow with gratitude and joy as we await your glorious return. Strengthen us in faith, that we may boldly proclaim your Gospel and live as ambassadors of your kingdom.

In Jesus' name, we pray. Amen.

www.ingramcontent.com/pod-product-compliance
Lightning Source LLC
Chambersburg PA
CBHW070942120626
46546CB00004B/1522